Dear,

Future Black Queen

Leslie Crawford

All rights reserved. No part of this book/publication may be reproduced, stored in a retrieval system, or transmitted in any form or by any means, electronic, mechanical, photocopying, recording, or otherwise; without written consent from both the author and publisher of Exposed Books Publishing, LLC, except for brief quotes used in reviews. For information regarding special discounts or bulk purchases, please contact Exposed Books Publishing at info@exposedbooks.com.

© 2020, by Leslie Crawford of Exposed Books Publishing, LLC

All rights reserved, including the right of reproduction in whole or in part of any form.

ISBN 978-1-7348081-4-8

Library of Congress Catalog Card Number 2020907810

Dear Future Black Queen

Written by: Leslie Crawford

Cover Design: Essence Jones

Printed in the United States of America

This book is dedicated to all of my future black queens. Keep your head up, princess. Queens nor princesses, never look down unless they're helping their fellow sister up.

Dear Future Black Queen,

To the young lady that stares in the mirror and thinks she's not pretty because of how dark her skin is. To the girl that hates going shopping because of how tall she is. This is for the princess that believes she's ugly because her hair is kinky and coarse. To the future black queen that thinks she's no good because no one tells her, I love you. For the young girl that thinks she has to be hood in order to be accepted. To the girl that doesn't believe God loves her because of the bad things that have happened in her life. To the young girl that made a bad choice, and no one will let it go. For the young lady that doesn't believe she is capable of being anything, she would like to be. This is for YOU. This book is for every black princess out there, no matter what you look like or have been through in life. THIS IS FOR YOU.

While you're reading this book, I want you to take yourself on a journey. A journey of faith, belief, self-love, affirmation, praise, love, acceptance, confidence, and, most of all, a journey of knowing you are a FUTURE BLACK QUEEN. This book is meant to be read daily, take your time.

In early 2020 it hit me that so many young girls don't understand the value of their life. I wanted to create something that will remind you daily of how important you are. My goal was to touch on various topics that most young black princesses go through, but no one really talks to them about it. There are some letters that I have written to you. There are poems where I'm speaking to you, and somewhere you are talking to yourself. I am taking you on a journey to becoming a FUTURE BLACK QUEEN.

# DEAR FUTURE BLACK QUEEN,
# IT'S YOUR TIME!

*Message for the day: I Love My Skin*

Dear Future Black Queen,

Your skin glows without needing the sun to shine.

Your skin brings out your beautiful eyes.

Your skin is a weapon to some, but we all know it's a gift from God that was not granted to everyone.

Your skin is smooth like a peach, but it'll never go rotten because you are sweet.

Never downplay how beautiful your skin is. Whether it's dark chocolate, caramel, mocha, or pecan, you are beautiful because beauty comes from within.

How did you feel before you read the message for today?

How did you feel after you read the message for today?

How can you be more confident in yourself?

Notes:

*Message for the day: I Am Somebody*

Dear Future Black Queen,

Who are they to say you are nobody?

Don't you know that you are somebody?

You are a princess, a queen in the making.

A black goddess that fills the world with her smile, and you don't have to fake it.

You don't have to be like the woman in the video.

You don't have to be the lady that wants to be put on a show.

You are special, you are divine, you were made in God's image, and that's no lie.

Be proud of who you are, and never fake it.

Stand up straight and show the world you are going to make it.

How did you feel before you read the message for today?

How did you feel after you read the message for today?

How can you be more confident in yourself?

Notes:

*Message for the day: I Will Always Love Me First*

Dear Future Black Queen,

You can't love them if you don't love you.

How do I know? This is what I used to do.

I would love everyone but never had enough for me.

I was broken and couldn't even see.

I couldn't see that I had to put me first.

I couldn't spread the love if I didn't love me first.

Before you start to wonder if you can, take a look in the mirror and say, "Yes, I can."

Yes, you can love yourself first; you are no good to anyone if you don't put yourself first.

Stand in the mirror and tell yourself every day, "I LOVE YOU."

Shout it to the world if you have to.

Spread love around, but make sure you keep a portion for you.

How did you feel before you read the message for today?

How did you feel after you read the message for today?

How can you be more confident in yourself?

Notes:

*Message for the day: Today Will Be Great Because I Am Alive*

Dear Future Black Queen,

Today will be a great day, just because you are great.

The world can't start until you wake up.

Did you know your life plays a big part?

A big part in how someone's day may go.

You never know how much joy you can bring just by saying hello.

Hello to the little girl that has lost her way.

Hello to the little boy that just wants to run away.

Your words have a major impact. Make sure you are not filling your mind with a bunch of bull crap.

Positivity goes a long way, spread love, and believe you are great.

Great in a world filled with foolishness, but you are the exception because of your greatness.

Always start your day believing it will be great.

You are the key to how your day will be shaped.

How did you feel before you read the message for today?

How did you feel after you read the message for today?

How can you be more confident in yourself?

Notes:

*Message for the day: I Love My Thick Natural Hair*

Dear Future Black Queen,

Let them stare.

Let them talk.

It's your right to wear your hair long or short.

Some don't understand the history of your hair.

For years we straightened it with the creamy crack.

Now we are clean and back on the right track.

You and your hair are both beautiful and strong.

Our hair is no longer at the mercy of those that did us wrong.

It's our choice of how we want to wear our hair.

Stop allowing people to make you feel bad.

What do you want?

A nice twist out.

Or an afro too.

What about some long flowing locs?

Or will a short natural cut satisfy you?

No matter the style or length, love your natural hair like you love your best friend.

How did you feel before you read the message for today?




How did you feel after you read the message for today?




How can you be more confident in yourself?




Notes:

*Message for the day: My Beauty Is Not Defined by My Looks*

Dear Future Black Queen,

Stand in the mirror, and what do you see?

Do you see just a person or a future queen?

In order for you to play your part, you must know your beauty is what sets you apart.

I'm not talking about the beauty everyone sees on the outside.

I'm talking about the beauty that you portray from the inside.

A queen treats other's right, and that only comes from the love you have hidden on the inside.

Don't focus too much on the outer layer.

That will only get you as far as a slow caterpillar.

Be the butterfly that is out of sight.

The butterfly that focuses on endurance, change, hope, and life.

Remember, it's not about what you see.

It's about how to treat yourself and the people you meet.

Your beauty is not defined by your looks.

How did you feel before you read the message for today?




How did you feel after you read the message for today?




How can you be more confident in yourself?




Notes:

*Message for the day: God Loves Me*

Dear Future Black Queen,

When you wake up this morning, there's something I want you to know.

Even when no one else tells you, God has love for you deep down in your soul.

It's not the kind of love from your parents.

It's the love that no matter what, you two are always on the up and up.

Love from your parents is great.

Knowing God loves you every day is never up for debate.

When the world seems to let you down, think about God's love and turn that frown upside down.

Smile, God Loves You.

How did you feel before you read the message for today?

How did you feel after you read the message for today?

How can you be more confident in yourself?

Notes:

*Message for the day: I Love Me More Today*

Dear Future Black Queen,

They say when you are on a plane, and there is an emergency, you should equip yourself with the oxygen mask first before you help anyone else. Why? How can you help someone if you're helpless? This letter today is to remind you that loving yourself more and more every day is a bonus in every way.

Is it easy to say we love someone else? How easy is it to say "I love you" to yourself and mean it?

Life will place many people in our lives. They will be people to help us and to love us. Most of these people will not stay for various reasons. The one person that will always be there to have your back and hold you up is the person that stares back at you in the mirror. You will always be the one person that walks with you every day and through everything. Stand in the mirror, starting today, and tell yourself, "I love you." Love yourself more and more every day. You are more than capable of falling in love with yourself first.

How did you feel before you read the message for today?

How did you feel after you read the message for today?

How can you be more confident in yourself?

Notes:

*Message for the day: I'm Not an Angry Black Girl*

Dear Future Black Queen,

One day I was talking to a young girl that was between 10 and 11 years old. We were having a general conversation about her conduct in class. She preceded to tell me that the reason she acts the way she does is because she's angry. Why did she think she was angry? Multiple adults told her she was an angry black girl.

My message to you today is not to allow anyone to label you as an angry black girl. So many princesses like you are hurting for various reasons. This does not make you angry or a girl with an attitude. This makes you human. Society has labeled us for way too long. Break those chains by being part of the beautiful black queens and princesses, that reject the enemy of anger and labeling. You are a beautiful and intelligent future queen.

        **YOU ARE NOT AN ANGRY BLACK GIRL.**

How did you feel before you read the message for today?

How did you feel after you read the message for today?

How can you be more confident in yourself?

Notes:

*Message for the day: Today I Will Make Great Choices*

Dear Future Black Queen,

Yesterday wasn't a good day.

You brushed everything off and went on about your day.

You went to sleep angry because you couldn't have your way.

What choices were made that caused you to feel this way?

Take a moment to think about it, so you can get yourself all the way straight.

You may have made a bad choice yesterday, but today is a new day.

You're going to make better choices because we don't want you to feel blue.

Look in the mirror and tell yourself, "I Love You."

How did you feel before you read the message for today?




How did you feel after you read the message for today?




How can you be more confident in yourself?




Notes:

*Message for the day: I am A Future Black Queen*

Dear Future Black Queen,

I am a future black queen.

Don't say it just to be seen.

I want you to say it because that's what you mean.

Stand up straight with your head held high.

Look them all in the face and show your black pride.

Any time you start to feel overwhelmed, remember who you are and straighten your crown

You are a future black queen.

How did you feel before you read the message for today?

How did you feel after you read the message for today?

How can you be more confident in yourself?

Notes:

*Message for the day: I Am Enough*

Dear Future Black Queen,

Today I want you to repeat "I am enough" anytime you feel the need to compete.

When there are times when you believe you have to be like the next girl in order to feel complete.

You are more than enough, and I hope you know it.

There's no one else like you on this earth, believe you are more than enough and that you're worth it.

How did you feel before you read the message for today?




How did you feel after you read the message for today?




How can you be more confident in yourself?




Notes:

*Message for the day: I Choose Me Today*

Dear Future Black Queen,

I want you to choose you today.

Choosing everyone else before yourself will only get in your way.

It's okay to help others, but only if you're able to help yourself.

What good are you to them, if you keep putting your goals on the shelf?

How will you ever be successful if you don't start doing things to better yourself?

I Choose Me isn't just a slogan; it's the way you live your life when you are chosen.

Chosen by God to do his work.

Chosen to put yourself first, then help everyone else with their work.

I want you to choose you today, then get on the path to help everyone else while you're on your way.

How did you feel before you read the message for today?

How did you feel after you read the message for today?

How can you be more confident in yourself?

Notes:

*Message for the day: Me Against Me*

Dear Future Black Queen,

It's easy to blame everyone else when things don't go my way.

But when I look in the mirror, it's only me that's standing in the way.

It's me against me, not the world as they say.

Before the world can stop me from being great, I have to give them permission to stand in my way.

You see, sometimes it's not everyone else that's holding me back, it's the same person that stares in my face and smiles back.

It's me against me, and I'm glad I finally noticed it.

Now I can move out of my own way and start on the path of being a dope sis.

How did you feel before you read the message for today?

How did you feel after you read the message for today?

How can you be more confident in yourself?

Notes:

*Message for the day: My Black Skin is Beautiful*

Dear Future Black Queen,

It doesn't matter if your skin is dark chocolate, cocoa brown, caramel or fudge, you are beautiful in your own way. Your skin is a representation of everything your ancestors went through for you to be here today. Don't hide behind products thinking it will make you prettier. Love who you are and the skin that you're in. Repeat after me, "My Black Skin Is Beautiful," and that's the end. The end of this conversation and the end of your lack of respect. Lack of respect for yourself and your smooth skin. Love who you are and understand your beautiful black skin will prevail in the end. My Skin is Beautiful.

How did you feel before you read the message for today?




How did you feel after you read the message for today?




How can you be more confident in yourself?




Notes:

*Message for the day: All of My Problems Have Solutions*

Dear Future Black Queen,

I remember when I would allow my problems to dominate my life. Something would happen, and I would think it was the end of the world. Today I want you to know you had a bad day, not a bad life. Every problem that you have encountered or will encounter, there's a solution to it. Take a deep look at the problem you're having and see how it can be fixed. It may not be able to be fixed today or tomorrow, but if there's a solution out there, I'm sure you'll conquer it. Don't allow a big or small problem to stress you out. Take a step back and remind yourself that you are more than a conqueror. You can handle anything that comes your way. There is a solution to every problem; you just have to take the time to find it.

How did you feel before you read the message for today?

How did you feel after you read the message for today?

How can you be more confident in yourself?

Notes:

*Message for the day: Opportunity*

Dear Future Black Queen,

This is my opportunity, you will see, for everyone that stood in my way and didn't believe in me.

This is my opportunity to show the world that I am a beautiful black girl.

A black girl that's not here just for show, but this is my opportunity to let everyone know what I am capable of.

I can be a doctor and heal the sick.

If I wanted to be a track star, I know I can make it to the Olympics.

They say being an artist doesn't pay much, but I can guarantee you that you'll be buying my work with your last buck.

They say being a teacher doesn't pay, for me, it's not about the money, but paving away.

This is my opportunity to show the world that no matter what, I am the future, and us black girls will rule the world.

How did you feel before you read the message for today?

How did you feel after you read the message for today?

How can you be more confident in yourself?

Notes:

*Message for the day: I'm Not Ghetto*

Dear Future Black Queen,

They think I'm ghetto because of where I live; I'm not ghetto because I know what lies ahead.

Do you think I'm ghetto because I speak loud?

Have you ever thought that I was practicing speaking in front of a crowd?

They label me as ghetto because of my speech, when the entire time, they are trying their best to be like me.

Society says I'm ghetto when I wear my hair in braids; now she's over there wearing them because it's trendy and she's getting paid.

You label me as ghetto, but I know better.

I'm someone that lives a life that you copy in order to make yours better.

It's easy to call me ghetto because of where I'm from.

If you took the time to get to know me, you'd know I'm not the one.

I'm not the one that allows others to label me.

I'm not ghetto because I am a future black queen.

How did you feel before you read the message for today?

How did you feel after you read the message for today?

How can you be more confident in yourself?

Notes:

*Message: I am Beautiful! Who Me? Yes, You!*

Dear Future Black Queen,

When you look in the mirror, what do you see?

Do you see someone that is fit to be a queen?

When you look in the mirror, I want you to know, you are beautiful inside and out, just look at your glow.

When someone says you are beautiful, don't turn around and ask, who me?

Say thank you, and most of all, please believe.

How did you feel before you read the message for today?




How did you feel after you read the message for today?




How can you be more confident in yourself?




Notes:

*Message: The Box*

Dear Future Black Queen,

There are people out there that will try to place you in a box. Please understand you are too intelligent to go along with that stupid plot. Those that try to put you in the box; it's only because they don't want you to succeed. They know you are unstoppable and destined to be great. The box is there to keep you in one place. As a future black queen, you are not meant to stay in one place. God created this world, so you can move around and not be stuck. Stuck in a place where everyone is going off of luck. Black women are the backbone of this world. You, too, will be part of the decision making in this world.

See, if you allow yourself to be placed in the box, we may miss out on you, showing us a lot. What if you could be the CEO of a bank? How about the teacher that each kid leans on for support? Have you thought about how your spoken word can change the world? If you're stuck in the box, none of these manifestations will be able to unfold. The president of the United States could be waiting for you. You could even be a lawyer which will allow you to speak your truth. The box is there, and they will try to place you in it, just walk past it and let them know future black queens are too powerful to fit in their box. Never allow anyone to put you inside of a box.

How did you feel before you read the message for today?

How did you feel after you read the message for today?

How can you be more confident in yourself?

Notes:

*Message: Black Girls Are Loud*

Dear Future Black Queen,

"Why are you so loud?" That's what they say. "You're loud and ghetto, please get out of my way."

Unfortunately, I have heard this most of my life about black girls and women. It's so hard to express ourselves without someone thinking we're just too loud. Do you silence yourself to please them? Will you stop speaking in your normal tone so that no one will look at you funny? What do you do when society says you're too loud? You keep talking. You have something to say, so don't silence your voice just for them to be okay. Don't see yourself as being loud; see yourself as being black and proud. Proud to use your voice for anything. Proud of who you are and not allowing anyone to stand in your way. The next time society tells you to quiet down, remember, you're a black girl that uses her voice, and it just comes across as loud.

How did you feel before you read the message for today?

How did you feel after you read the message for today?

How can you be more confident in yourself?

Notes:

*Message: I Will Not Compare Myself to Anyone Else*

Dear Future Black Queen,

How often have you watched a friend or classmate and wished you were like them? You compared every part of you to them. You have sized up your hair against theirs. You constantly compare your life to them. Is she smarter than me? I think she's prettier than me. She definitely dresses better than me. Her family has more money than mine. Her skin is not like mine; in fact, it's much prettier than mine. Your life was assigned to you for a reason. Stop comparing yourself to others because you don't know what they go through. You don't know if she's living a rough life at home or if it's easy going. Do you know if her family helps her with her homework? Or do they tell her to figure it out on her own? What if she goes days without seeing a parent, but they shower her with gifts to make up for it? What if the pretty clothes are to cover up what she doesn't want you to see? Maybe she wears makeup to hide a lot of things. It's easy to sit down and start comparing yourself to others, but remember you don't know what someone else is going through when you never walked in their shoes. She might be thinking she wished she was you.

How did you feel before you read the message for today?

How did you feel after you read the message for today?

How can you be more confident in yourself?

Notes:

*Message: Today I Am A Leader*

Dear Future Black Queen,

This letter is very dear to me because I remember when I wanted to be a follower. When I was in middle school, there was a group of popular girls. I knew them because we were all from the same community, but I wasn't part of the popular clique. I wanted to dress like these girls. I begged my mom to let me wear my hair in a certain style because they had it. I wanted to go to parties like them. I basically wanted to follow them around all because I wanted to be accepted.

Today, I am glad everything was what I wanted to do but didn't do it. Being a follower will get you know where. It only leaves you inhaling their dust because you're walking behind them. When you follow others, you always find yourself one step behind. You will never be the first one in line. Your next move will always depend on what they do next. Who wants their life based off what someone else will do next? You don't want to base your every move off how someone else will choose. Before you think about being a follower, look at what comes with it. Being a leader may be harder, but it's worth it.

How did you feel before you read the message for today?

How did you feel after you read the message for today?

How can you be more confident in yourself?

Notes:

*Message: I Forgive Myself for the Mistakes I Have Made*

Dear Future Black Queen,

I can guarantee you; you will make mistakes. There will be mistakes that others can't forgive you for, and sometimes that's okay. We all make mistakes because life is about learning. Learning how to navigate through the ups and downs. When you make a mistake, don't look at it as a failure. Instead, look at it as a lesson being taught. Don't be too hard on yourself because you are human too. Mistakes are one of the biggest lessons in life, but the answer is always forgiving yourself. Never dwell on the mistake because it happens to everyone. Instead, look at how you can grow from it and avoid it in the future. Starting today, forgive yourself for every mistake you have made. Forgive yourself for being angry with yourself. Forgive yourself for not getting it right the first time around. Forgive yourself for all of the drama you put yourself through. Forgive yourself for the time you yelled. Forgive yourself for disobeying your parents. Forgive yourself for not listening to your teacher. You are allowed to make a mistake; the key is not to repeat the mistake. You're at the stage in life where sometimes things don't make sense. You're confused, which often leads to a confused reaction. It's okay because it was just a bad day, not a bad life. Forgive yourself!

How did you feel before you read the message for today?

How did you feel after you read the message for today?

How can you be more confident in yourself?

Notes:

*Message: I Accept Who I Am*

Dear Future Black Queen,

I accept who I am! As you say those words out loud, do you really mean it? Do you accept how dark your skin is? Do you accept the pimples that are starting to appear? Are you accepting how tall and skinny you are? Have you learned to accept that your weight is not who you are? Are you okay with having short thick hair? Or do you prefer a perm because that's what everyone else is wearing? Are you fine with not wearing the latest clothes? Are you okay with you, just being you? It's easy to read these questions and say yes, but can you honestly say, "I accept who I am, and I'm not changing for anyone?" Accepting who you are is the first step. The first step to discovering the real you. It's so easy to fall into the trap, the trap of not accepting yourself and all of your mess. None of us are perfect, and we each have our ways, but accept who you are to help make this world a better place.

How did you feel before you read the message for today?

How did you feel after you read the message for today?

How can you be more confident in yourself?

Notes:

*Message: Chin Up*

Dear Future Black Queen,

Hey, pretty lady, why do you keep your head down?

There's nothing down there, but the ground.

I know life can be hard, and that's no lie.

Sometimes you have to hold your head up high and kiss those tears goodbye.

When things tend to get hard, remember how strong you are.

When things get tough, and you can't see your way through, look towards the sky, and remember who created you.

Life will be full of ups and downs.

Keep your chin up and try not to frown.

You were born a fighter, and sometimes it may burn.

Anything that comes out of the fire ends up burning brighter.

So, keep your chin up, and your head held high.

Always look forward to the ending prize.

How did you feel before you read the message for today?

How did you feel after you read the message for today?

How can you be more confident in yourself?

Notes:

*Message: It Is Enough to Do My Best*

Dear Future Black Queen,

Is it enough to do your best? You put your all into it, and everything turned out to be an ugly mess.

This happens all the time. You studied hard for a test, but you didn't get the grade you wanted. You watched that YouTube video on how to make something, but when you attempted it, it wasn't a success. Before you start to come down on yourself, ask yourself if you tried your best. Did you put your all into it, or did you start to slack? You have two options: You can try again and see what can be improved. Or you can walk away and feel good about it because you did try your best. When things seem not to go your way, stop and think if you did your best. If you did your best, let it be. You did what you were supposed to do, and the rest is history. It is enough to do your best, even if the results don't turn out the way you want.

How did you feel before you read the message for today?

How did you feel after you read the message for today?

How can you be more confident in yourself?

Notes:

*Message: I Will Make A Difference*

Dear Future Black Queen,

I will make a difference in everything I do.

I'm the future of this world, and I must believe in what I will do.

I will use my voice in order to be heard.

I can be a lawyer to fight for injustice.

I can be the judge that has the lawyers back.

I can be a teacher that will teach all of the kids how to do math.

I can be a scientist to help find cures.

I can be an entrepreneur that will open doors.

Open doors to help employ others so they can continue to soar.

I can be a mentor, pastor, advocate, or anything else I want to be.

The key is to make a difference for my community.

No matter what I decide to do, I will make a difference in the future for my crew and me.

How did you feel before you read the message for today?

How did you feel after you read the message for today?

How can you be more confident in yourself?

Notes:

*Message: I Will Stand Up for What I Believe In*

Dear Future Black Queen,

Either I will stand or fall.

I rather stand up for what I believe in, especially when I know I'm not wrong.

I don't know everything, but I do know this, if I don't stand for something, I could end up falling for a bunch of mess.

I believe in human rights, rights for blacks.

I will fight for us because no one else will have our backs.

I am a future black queen, that will fight every day to make sure my people are heard and seen.

My ancestors fought a good fight.

I will continue to fight with all of my might.

I can't let them down; they are the ones that afforded me the opportunity to wear this crown.

I will stand up for what I believe in.

How did you feel before you read the message for today?




How did you feel after you read the message for today?




How can you be more confident in yourself?




Notes:

*Message: Today I Choose to Be Confident in The Skin I Am In*

Dear Future Black Queen,

Today I choose to be confident in the skin I am in.

It doesn't matter if I have pimples growing on my face, I'm still a winner within.

Today I choose to be confident in the skin I am in.

Someone fought for me to have the luxury of this beautiful black skin.

Today I choose to be confident in the skin I am in.

The love I have for myself outweighs all other thoughts about who they think I am.

Today I choose to be confident in the skin I am in.

I am a future black queen; therefore, I will win.

How did you feel before you read the message for today?




How did you feel after you read the message for today?




How can you be more confident in yourself?




Notes:

Thank you for taking the time to read Dear Future Black Queen. I pray that you have gained more knowledge and love about yourself. I pray that you are proud of who you are. I pray that you will embrace your flaws and understand we all have flaws. Remember to keep your chin up, a smile on your face, and love in your heart.

# DEAR FUTURE BLACK QUEEN, IT'S YOUR TIME!

www.ingramcontent.com/pod-product-compliance
Lightning Source LLC
LaVergne TN
LVHW021622080426
835510LV00019B/2726